Xhosa
English
South Sotho
Afrikaans

A publication of the Anti-bias Project
EARLY LEARNING RESOURCE UNIT

'Jakkals trou met Wolf se vrou'

…yanetha kodwa kukho ilanga. U-Achmat uthi,
…Jdyakalashe utshata nomfazi kaMfolufo."

It is raining but the sun is shining. Achmat says,
"Jackal is getting married to Wolf's wife."

…ıla e ya na empa letsatsi le tjhabile. Achmat o re,
…Phokojwe o nyala mosadi wa Phiri."

Dit reën maar die son skyn.
Achmat sê, "Jakkals trou met Wolf se vrou."

'O nkena hanong'

USis Mimi uthi, "Suk' uthetha ndithetha. Unditsibela emlonyeni."

Sis Mimi says, "Don't talk while I'm speaking. You are jumping into my mouth."

Sis Mimi o re, "O se ke wa bua ha ke bua. O nkena hanong."

Sis Mimi sê, "Moenie praat as ék praat nie. Jy spring in my mond in."

'Ndikhatywe yinkawu'

JMandla ulambile. Uthi, "Ndiph'ukutya!
Ndikhatywe yinkawu."

Mandla is very hungry. He says, "Give me food!
t feels as if I'm being kicked by a monkey."

Mandla o lapile. O re, "Mphe dijo! Ekare ke
rahilwe ke tshwene."

Mandla is baie honger. Hy sê, "Gee vir my kos!
Dit voel asof 'n aap my skop."

'Don't get in a stew'

USaira akazifumani izihlangu zakhe. UMama uthi,
"Zola. Sukuzifaka kwi-stew."

Saira can't find her shoe. Her mother says, "Stay cool. Don't get in a stew."

Saira ha a fumane seeta sa hae. Mme o re,
"Kgoba matshwafo. Se kene ka setjhung."

Saira kry nie haar skoen nie. Haar ma sê,
"Bly kalm. Moenie in die bredie klim nie."

UWilma ubukela abamelwane.
Uthi, "Balwa okwekati nenja."

Wilma watches the neighbours.
She says, "They fight like cat and dog."

Wilma o shebile baahisani. O re, "Ba lwana sa ntja le katse."

Wilma hou die bure dop. Sy sê, "Hulle baklei soos kat en hond."

'Hulle baklei soos kat en hond'

'Uzinqikela ilitye elinembovane'

UNomsa udlala ngematshisi. u-Amos uthi, "Uzinqikela ilitye elinembovane."

Nomsa is playing with matches. Amos says,
"You are turning over a stone with ants for yourself."

Nomsa o bapala ka mollo. Amos o re, "O iphetolela lejwe le nang le marwana."

Nomsa speel met vuurhoutjies. Amos sê, "Jy rol 'n klip om
met miere vir jouself."

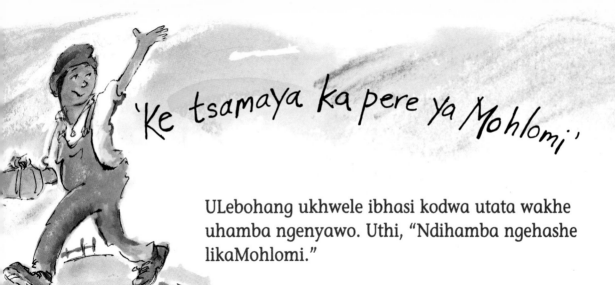

'Ke tsamaya ka pere ya Mohlomi'

ULebohang ukhwele ibhasi kodwa utata wakhe uhamba ngenyawo. Uthi, "Ndihamba ngehashe likaMohlomi."

ebohang goes by bus but her father goes on foot. He says,
I'm going on Mohlomi's horse."

ebohang o tsamaya ka bese empa ntatae o tsamaya ka maoto.
Ntatae o re, "Ke tsamaya ka pere ya Mohlomi."

ebohang ry met die bus maar haar pa stap te voet.
Iy sê, "Ek ry op Mohlomi se perd."

'Ek skrik nie vir koue pampoen nie'

Umhlobo kaLisa woyika impuku.
ULisa uthi, "Kutheni usoyika nje?
Andoyik'ithanga elibandayo."

Lisa's friend is frightened of a little mouse. Lisa says,
"Why are you scared? I'm not scared of cold pumpkin."

Motswalle wa Lisa o tshoswa ke tweba. Lisa o re, "O tshohileng? Ha ke
tshoswe ke mokopu o batang."

Lisa se vriend skrik vir 'n muisie. Lisa sê,
"Waarom skrik jy? Ek skrik nie vir koue pampoen nie."

'He's pulling your leg'

Ndisoloko ndikholelwa kumabali agezayo kaPeter. U-Anti Farieda uthi, "Akumboni? Ukutsala ngomlenze."

I always believe Peter's crazy stories. Aunty Farieda says, "Can't you see? He's just pulling your leg."

Ke atisa ho dumela dipale tsa Peter tse makatsang. Malome Farieda o re, "Ha o bone? O mpa a o hula ka leoto."

Ek glo altyd Peter se lawwe stories. Antie Farieda sê, "Kan jy nie sien nie? Hy trek net jou been."

'Bana ba tadi ba tsebana ka mereto'

UVusi ufumana umhlobo. UMnu da Silva uthi, "Abantwana bempuku bazana ngemigca yabo."

Vusi finds a friend. Mr da Silva says, "The children of the fieldmouse know each other by their stripes."

Vusi o fumano motswalle. Mong da Silva o re, "Bana ba tadi ba tsebana ka mereto."

Vusi kry 'n maat. Mnr Da Silva sê, "Die veldmuis se kinders ken mekaar aan hul strepe."

'Ikati ilele eziko'

Akukho kutya namhlanje.
UTata Elias uthi, "Ikati ilele eziko."

There is no food to cook today. Tata Elias says, "The cat is lying in the fireplace."

Ha ho dijo tse phehwang kajeno. Ntate Elias o re,
"Katse e robetse ifo."

Vandag is daar geen kos te kook nie. Tata Elias sê,
"Die kat lê in die vuurmaakplek."

'It's raining cats and dogs'

Imvula iyagalela. UMarie uthi, "Kunethela iikati nezinja."

It is pouring with rain. Marie says, "It's raining cats and dogs."

Pula e ya tsholoha. Marie o re, "Ho na ya dikatse le dintja."

Dit reën hard. Marie sê, "Dit reën katte en honde."

'Jy eet lang tand'

Wisdom akalithandi ikhaphetshu. UGogo uthi, "Utya ngamazinyo amade."

Wisdom doesn't like cabbage. Granny says, "You are eating with long teeth."

Wisdom ha a rate khabetjhe. Nkgono o re, "O ja ka meno a matelele."

Wisdom hou nie van kool nie. Gogo sê, "Jy eet lang tand."

'Yinyoka nesele'

ULulama noBoetie bayaxabana.
UDudu uthi, "Yinyoka nesele."

Lulama and Boetie do not get on. Dudu says,
"They are a snake and a frog."

Lulama le Boetie ha ba utlwane. Dudu o re, "Ke noha le senqanqane."

Lulama en Boetie kom nie oor die weg nie.
Dudu sê, "Hulle is 'n slang en 'n padda."

Xa abantu bencedana, bahlambana izandla.

When people help one another it is like hands washing each other.

Ha batho ba thusana, matsoho a hlatswana.

As mense mekaar help is dit soos die een hand was die ander.

MATSOHO A HLATSWANA

Illustrations:	Trish de Villiers
Concept:	Reviva Schermbrucker
Text:	Reviva Schermbrucker and Trish de Villiers
Consulting team:	Thikam Pillay, Jos Horwitz, Linda Biersteker and Carol Smith
Research:	Jane Parry
Layout:	Simon Ford
Translations and proof-reading:	Blossom Ngwevela, Mimi Bethela, Ros Herbert, Isaac Leshoro, Mmamie Kodisang and Mpai Ramathe
Sponsors:	Rockefeller Brothers Fund and Royal Netherlands Embassy

Copyright © 1997 Early Learning Resource Unit 19 Flamingo Crescent, Lansdowne 7780

ISBN 1 875 069 21 6
A production of the Anti-bias project of the Early Learning Resource Unit

Printed and bound by Tandym Print